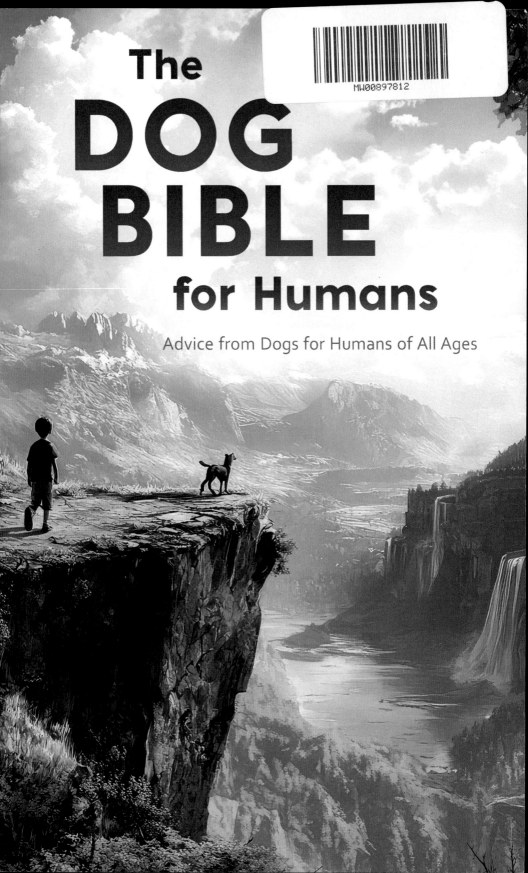

The
DOG
BIBLE
for Humans

Advice from Dogs for Humans of All Ages

www.audreylevy.com
audrey@audreylevy.com

Cover and interior design by Frame25 Productions

Cover and interior photos by
Meta AI, Midjourney, and
Shutterstock (GraphicsRF.com, YG Studio, and Audrey1005)

Pacific Style Books
P.O. Box 10358
Marina Del Rey, CA 90295

Pacific Style Books are available at special discounts for bulk purchases, sales promotion, fund-raising, or educational purposes. Special editions can be created to specifications. For details, contact Special Sales Department, Pacific Style Publishers, P.O. Box 10358, Marina Del Rey, CA 90295.

ISBN 979-8-338895-91-7

Printed in the United States of America
First Edition—September 2024

This book is dedicated to the dogs
who allowed me to be their person:

Stoshie

Silvi

Corky

Kelly

Louie

and

To the Persons, who allowed me to grow:

My Parents: Albert and Julie Levy

My Biological Brothers: Larry and Ken Levy

My Chosen Brothers: Evan Landy and Bill Flaxman

My Cousins: Shoshanna Smith and Louise Schneider

My Mentors: Dr. Eugene Landy and Dr. Sol Samuels

My Significant Others: Dr. James Spencer & Michael Charles Way

~ Thank you ~

Introduction

In the beginning . . . there was a parallel universe in which a group lived, who looked like the Earth species called a Dog, and they created the Dog Bible, which is **Basic Instructions Before Leaving Earth!**

Please note here that also on Earth, the human species, for the most part, has decided that God created and runs things and that God is most definitely Dog spelled backward . . . not to mention that, in my mind, God stands for a **Group Of Dogs!**

Now, picture a King's Domain—a castle with landscaping galore—beautiful grounds, including gardens, fountains,

and even a labyrinth because we can't forget having some-place in which the white mice from *Hitchhikers in the Galaxy* can play, so that we "Don't panic!"

The King is an absentminded scientist who looks just like a very handsome alpha male German Shepherd. He wears a Yankees baseball cap with jeans, T-shirt and sneakers, bifo-cals on his long nose, and he stares at a big old beaker full of

the purest, brightest batch of energy that any of us has ever seen. It belongs in Disney's *Fantasia* movie, that is how fan-tastic this beaker of energy looks to the naked eye!

The King's five-year-old daughter, Grace, came into her father's laboratory. "Hi, Daddy, "What are you doing?"

There but for the Grace of God Go I . . .

"Well, honey," said the King, "I am trying to think of something original to do with this."

The King put Grace up on the counter so that she could see into the beaker. She immediately reached out to touch the glass, mesmerized by the constant gentle movement of the ball of energy that was a beautiful diamond-like light.

"What is it, Daddy?" Her own beautiful brown puppy eyes were reflected in the gleam of the light.

"It's life, sweetheart. It's what we're made of. It's pure energy. It's what we all are."

"What does *o-rig-i-nal* mean, Daddy?"

"Something that's never been done before, sweetheart."

"Never, Daddy."

"Nope. Never, ever."

"What would that be like Daddy?"

The King turned his daughter's angle on the counter. "Here. Look at this hologram of the planet Earth."

Dogs called us "Earth."

The puppy looked at the blue and green planet such a long distance away.

The King said to Grace, "You see, honey, that planet Earth has water and oxygen on it. I'm wondering what would happen if we threw some of that energy from the beaker . . ."

The King pointed out toward the blue and green planet, and said, ". . . down there.

Grace said, "I bet life would grow, Daddy!"

"Do you think so, sweetheart?"

"That would be o-rig-i-nal. Wouldn't it, Daddy?"

The King laughed, "Out of the mouths of babes! Yes, I'd have to say that if we could create life on another planet . . . Yes, that would be quite original. Okay, let's see what happens!"

What is the secret to life?

"Woof! [*ears perked up*] Oh, human friend! The secret to life is ... *panting* ... to chase the ball, not the worries! *Wagging tail...*

Live in the moment, sniff out the good stuff, and always, always keep your tail wagging! *Slurp...* And remember, belly rubs are the key to happiness! *Sigh...* Now, throw the ball already!"

Or, in a more concise doggy wisdom:

"Chase joy, not stress. Sniff love, not fear. Wag more, worry less."

How do I live simply?

"Easy! *Panting...* Here's how:

- Chase one ball at a time.

- Sniff the same spot, find new smells.

- Nap often, dream always.

- Worry less, wag more.

- Love unconditionally (especially treats).

- Play like no one's watching (they're not, they're on their phones).

- Find joy in the little things (like squeaky toys).

- Always come back to your pack.

Simple, right? *Wags tail...* Now, throw the ball, human! Focus on the fetch. Forget the fuss."

How do I love generously?

"Easy peasy! *Slurp*... Here's how:

- Love with your whole heart (and tongue)

- Give snuggles freely (even to strangers).

- Share your toys (and treats, if you must).

- Forgive quickly (they didn't mean to step on your paw).

- Listen with your ears (and your heart).

- Be present (no distractions, just belly rubs).

- Show affection (even when they're not expecting it).

And remember, love is like a game of fetch—it's meant to be shared! Love like you're licking a face—freely, sloppily, and with all your heart."

How do I care deeply?

"That's my specialty! *Nuzzles*... Here's how:

- Be present (I'll be right by your side).

- Listen with your heart (I hear you, even when you're not talking).

- Show physical affection (nuzzles, licks, and snuggles).

- Be loyal (you're my pack, I've got your back).

- Anticipate needs (I'll bring you my favorite toy, just in case).

- Forgive easily (you forgot my walk? No worries, I still love you).

- Celebrate milestones (*Woof! Woof!* You're home!).

- Offer comfort (my fur is your safe space).

Caring deeply is like a never-ending belly rub—it's all about the love and attention! Care like you're licking a wound—gently, patiently, and with all your love."

How do I speak kindly?

"That's my language! *Humming*... Here's how:

- Use a gentle tone (soft voice, like when you're giving treats).

- Be clear and simple (no complex sentences, just straightforward love).

- Listen actively (I'll tilt my head, you do the same).

- Avoid harsh words (no yelling, it hurts my ears ... and heart).

- Show empathy (if I'm whining, you comfort me).

- Use positive reinforcement (good boy, good girl, works wonders!).

- Be patient (I'll learn, just give me time and treats).

Speaking kindly is all about the gentle touch and loving intention! Speak kindly, as if every word is a treat."

When loved ones come home, always run to greet them. Why?

"Oh boy, oh boy! *Tail wags furiously* . . . You want to know why I always run to greet you when you come home? Well, here's the thing:

- I've missed you so much! *Panting . . .* You're my pack, my family, my everything!

- I love the excitement of reunions! It's like a big ol' party in my heart!

- I need to make sure you're okay! I've got to check your scent, your energy, your everything!

- I want to show you love and affection! It's my way of saying, 'I'm so happy you're home!'

- I've been waiting for this moment all day! It's the highlight of my day, every day!

Let's be honest . . . *sniffing . . .* I also love the attention, the treats, and the belly rubs that come with greeting you at the door! So, that's why I always run to greet you when you come home. It's just my way of saying, 'I love you, and I'm so happy you're mine!'"

Never pass up the opportunity to go for a joyride. Why?

"It's a dog's life, and I wouldn't have it any other way! Here's why:

- Life is short, and sniffing is forever! You never know when the next adventure will come along!

- The wind in my fur, the sun on my back, and the thrill of the unknown is the best feeling in the world!

- Joyrides are the best way to make memories with my favorite humans! *Gives you a big, slobbery grin . . .*

- You never know what amazing smells you'll discover or what fascinating things you'll see!

- It's a doggone good time, and you shouldn't miss out!

So, never pass up a joyride! *Barks . . .*"

Allow the experience of fresh air and the wind in your face to be pure ecstasy. Why?

"Why wouldn't I? Every breeze carries the scent of adventure, and the wind is like a thousand new stories swirling around me. It's a rush of pure joy! There's nothing better than feeling the world on my face, fur ruffling in the wind, and just living in that moment.

- The wind in my fur is like a thousand tiny scratches behind my ears—it's absolute bliss! *Tilts head back and lets out a contented sigh...*

- Fresh air fills my nose with all the amazing smells of the world!

- It's like a big, exciting adventure for my senses!

- Feeling the wind in my face makes me feel *alive!* *Spins around in circles, tail wagging wildly...*

- It's the best feeling in the world. I wish I could bottle it up and sniff it all day!

Fresh air and wind in your face is not just nice—it's *ecstasy!*"

Take naps. Why?

"Why not? Then I can dream about all the amazing things I'll sniff and chase when I wake up! Plus, a cozy spot in the sun is just too good to resist. *Twitches nose...*

- Napping is the best way to recharge my battery! *Curls up...*

- It's like a mini-vacation from all the hard work of being cute and playful! *Curls into a ball.*

- Napping is the best way to avoid getting into trouble (like eating a shoe or two ... oops)! *Whispers...*

- It's the perfect excuse to snooze the day away and let my humans do all the work! *Stretches and yawns...*

- Napping makes me feel like the king of the castle (or at least the king of the couch)! *Claims the spot...*

Napping is not just necessary—it's a doggy duty! *Wags tail and snuggles down..."*

Stretch before rising. Why?

"Stretching feels so good! It wakes up my muscles, and helps me get ready to move. It's like a big, happy yawn for my body.

- It helps me shake off the sleepies and get ready for adventure! *Shakes paws…*

- Stretching makes me feel like a brand new pup, ready to take on the day! *Stretches happily…*

- It's the best way to loosen up my furry muscles and get ready for all the running, jumping, and playing! *Flexes…*

- Plus, it's a great excuse to take my time and not rush into the day—after all, stretching is very important business! *Stretches again…*

Stretching before rising is a doggy must-do! *Gives you a big, slobbery grin…*"

How can I run, romp, and play daily?

"Wake up early and stretch! Get those juices flowing and shake off that sleep! *Stretches*...

- Find a buddy! Whether it's a human or a furry friend, having someone to play with makes it way more fun!

- Get outside! Sniff out some fresh air and find a place to run around. The park, the backyard, or even the beach—anywhere is paw-fect!

- Play, play, play! Chase balls, sticks, or just chase each other around. It's the best exercise ever!

- Take breaks, of course! We dogs need our beauty sleep too, you know. *Plops down*...

- Make it a routine! Set aside time each day for play-time. My humans call it 'exercise,' but I call it *fun*!

- And, most importantly, don't forget the *belly rubs*! They're the best reward after a long day of play!

There you have it! Follow these doggy tips, and you'll be running, romping, and playing like a pro in no time! *Rolls over*..."

Thrive on attention and let people touch you. Why?

"It's my nature! Dogs are pack animals, and we crave connection and affection from our pack so that we feel loved, calm and connected—that's you, human!

- Attention feels amazing! Belly rubs, ear scratches, and squeaky toys stimulate my senses and make me feel alive!

- Touch is comforting! Physical contact releases oxytocin, the 'cuddle hormone,' which calms me and strengthens our bond.

- It's a survival thing! In the wild, dogs that got attention from their pack were more likely to get food and protection. Old habits die hard, I guess!

- I love being a part of the family! When you give me attention and touch, I feel included and loved. It's the best feeling!

- It reduces stress! Attention and touch can calm my nerves and distract me from scary things like thunderstorms or vet visits.

Let's be honest . . . I'm a bit of an attention-seeker! I love being the center of attention—it's just so much fun!"

Avoid biting when a simple growl will do. Why?

"Biting hurts! I don't want to hurt my humans or friends. They give me treats and belly rubs, and I love them!

- Growling is enough! A good growl can warn them to back off without causing harm. It's like saying, 'Hey, personal space, please!'

- Biting can lead to trouble! It's my go-to warning sign. If I bite, I might get in trouble, and that means no more treats or playtime. No thank you!

- Growling is more flexible! I can growl softly to warn someone or growl louder to really make my point. Biting is just too extreme!

- It's better communication! Growling tells humans exactly what I'm feeling, whereas biting can be misinterpreted. I want to be clear, not confusing! *Tilts head...*

- I want to be a good dog! Biting is not good dog behavior. I want to make my humans proud and get those tasty rewards! *Licks lips...*

Growling is more natural in the wild. It's just what we do!"

On warm days, stop to lie on your back on the grass. Why?

"It's blissfully cool! The grass is like a refreshing carpet beneath me, soothing my fur and skin.

- I can soak up the sun! Lying on my back lets me bask in the warmth. It seeps into my bones. It's like a natural massage!

- It's a great way to relax! The warmth and comfort of the grass lull me into a peaceful snooze. I'm a dog, after all—napping is my joy!

- I can sniff the world! From this position, I can smell all the fascinating scents wafting by. It's like having my own personal fragrance buffet!

- It's a social thing! When I lie on my back, I'm inviting the world to come and give me belly rubs. It's the universal dog signal for 'scratch my tummy, please!'

It's just plain fun! Rolling onto my back and wriggling around on the grass is the best feeling. I'm a dog—I'm meant to enjoy the simple things!

On hot days, drink lots of water and lie under a shady tree. Why?

"Staying hydrated is crucial, especially when it's hot. I need water to keep my tongue wet and my tail wagging!

- Shade is my best friend! Direct sunlight can be overwhelming, but under a tree, it's cool and comfy. I can observe the world without getting heatstroke.

- It's a temperature thing! Trees provide the perfect canopy to regulate my body temperature. I can stay cool and relaxed, even when the sun is blazing.

- From under the tree, I can keep an eye on everything happening around me. Squirrels, birds, and even the occasional cat… it's like having my own personal TV!

- It's a doggy self-care thing! Taking care of myself on hot days is essential. Drinking water and resting in the shade helps me avoid overheating and feeling miserable.

My humans will thank me! If I stay cool and hydrated, I'll be a happier pup. That means more play time for me!"

When you're happy, dance around, and wag your entire body. Why?

"I just can't help it! When I'm excited or joyful, my whole body wants to join in on the fun! It's like my happiness is bursting out of me!

- It's the best way to express myself! As a dog, I don't have words, but I have movement. Dancing and wagging my body tells the world exactly how I'm feeling—happy, carefree, and full of energy!

- It's contagious! When I dance around, I can see my humans smiling and laughing. It's like we're sharing the happiness together!

- It's a stress reliever! When I'm feeling anxious or overwhelmed, a good dance session shakes it all off. I'm like, 'Wag, wag, wag—worries gone!'

- It's just plain fun! I mean, have you ever seen a dog dance? It's the most fun you can have on four legs! I'm like a furry little ballerina!

Dancing around and wagging my entire body is my happy language."

How can I delight in the simple joy of a long walk?

"Leave your worries behind! Don't bring your stress or anxiety on our walk. Just be present, like I am!

- Take your time! Don't rush. Sniff, explore, and enjoy the sights and sounds. I do!

- Get curious! Ask me questions, like "What's that smell?" or "What's up ahead?" I'll show you!

- Be present in the moment! Don't stare at that small rectangle thingy (you know, your phone). Look at me, look at nature, and enjoy the experience!

- Let me lead! Sometimes, I know the best route or the most interesting smells. Trust me, I've got this!

- Enjoy the little things! Watch me chase a leaf or bark at a bird. It's the simple things that make life paw-some!

- Take breaks! We don't have to walk the whole time. Let's sit, relax, and enjoy the view together!

Make it a game! Turn our walk into a treasure hunt, a sniffing adventure, or a fun exploration!"

How can I be loyal?

"Be present! Always be there for your pack, whether it's your human family or your furry friends. I'm always by my human's side!

- Keep your pack protected, safe and happy. I bark to alert my humans of danger and snuggle them when they're sad.

- Be consistent! Show up with a wagging tail and a loving heart. My humans know they can count on me!

- Communicate clearly! Use body language and vocal cues to let your pack know how you're feeling. I whimper when I need attention and kiss when I'm happy!

- Forgive and forget! Don't hold grudges. If my human accidentally steps on me, I forgive them and move on.

- Show affection! Snuggle, lick, and cuddle with your pack. Physical touch is key to loyalty and love!

- Be patient! Sometimes, my humans get busy or stressed. I wait calmly for them.

Stand by your pack! Through thick and thin, good times and bad, I stand by my humans. They're my everything!"

How can I never pretend to be something I'm not?

"You want to know how to be your authentic self? Here's my doggy advice:

- Be honest! If I'm tired, I sleep. If I'm hungry, I whine. I don't pretend to be full when I'm not!

- Don't try to be someone else! I'm a dog, and I love being a dog. I don't try to be a cat or a human. I'm me, and that's paw-some!

- Embrace your quirks! I have floppy ears and a wagging tail. They're part of who I am, and I love them!

- Don't hide your feelings! If I'm excited, I bark. If I'm scared, I whimper. I don't pretend to be brave when I'm not!

- Be loyal to yourself! I don't try to impress others by being someone I'm not. I stay true to myself and my pack!

Let your fur down! Okay, not literally, but be yourself. Don't try to put on a mask. I'm a dog and I'm proud of it!"

If what you want lies buried, dig until you find it. How can I persevere?

"Sniff out your goal! I use my nose to find what I want. You can use your instincts to find what you're looking for.

- Start digging! Don't be afraid to get your paws dirty. Take the first step towards your goal. Keep going!

- Don't give up! I don't stop digging until I find that bone. Don't stop until you reach your goal.

- Use your pack! I often have my human friends help me dig. Ask for help when you need it.

- Take breaks! I take a nap when I'm tired. You can rest too, but don't forget to keep digging!

- Celebrate small wins! I wag my tail when I find a small bone. You can celebrate your small victories too!

- Keep your nose to the ground! Stay focused, and don't get distracted.

Remember, if what you want lies buried, dig until you find it! I do, and you can too!"

When someone is having a bad day, be silent, sit close by, and nuzzle them gently. Why?

"Silence is golden! My humans don't want me to bark or whine when they're feeling down.

- Presence is everything! I snuggle close to my humans to let them know I'm there for them. It's comforting to have someone nearby who cares.

- Physical touch is awesome! A gentle nuzzle or lick on the hand can calm my humans down and make them feel loved. It's like a big hug from me.

- I can sense when my humans are feeling sad or stressed. I may not know what's wrong, but I know they need comfort and companionship.

- By being silent, sitting close, and nuzzling them gently, I can help them feel better. It's what pack members do for each other!

Plus, it's not just about my humans—sometimes I need comfort too! And when I do, my humans are there for me, just like I'm there for them. It's a doggy-human bond thing!"

How can I love unconditionally and forgive frequently?

"Unconditional love and forgiveness are my expertise!

- Love without judgment: I don't care if my human had a bad day or made a mistake. I wag my tail and give them a big kiss anyway!

- Focus on the present: I don't dwell on past mistakes or grudges. I live in the moment and enjoy the time with my human.

- Forgive and forget: I don't hold grudges. If my human accidentally steps on my paw, I yelp, but then I forgive and move on.

- Show affection freely: I shower my human with love and affection, no matter what. I'm like a furry love machine!

I do this because I know my human loves me unconditionally too! They feed me, walk me, and give me belly rubs, even when I'm being a bit stinky. So, I return the favor and love them just the same. It's a doggy-human love loop! Remember, my humans, I love you more than treats and walks combined!"

Epilogue

We're all going to the same place, and our dogs are there waiting for us, along with all the other animals . . .

So, we'll see you at the Rainbow Bridge.

12850052R00036